SEA SALT

LEARNING

THE COMMUNITY BUILDER GUIDEBOOK

ABOUT MY GUIDEBOOKS

This is one of a series of Guidebooks which, together, form my exploration notes for various aspects of the Social Age.

They form a diverse and evolving body of work, growing directly out of my primary writing, and research, on the blog at www.julianstodd.wordpress.com and www.SeaSaltLearning.com.

They are all written to be under 10,000 words, allowing them to be read fast!

I include sections for 'What you need to know', and 'What you need to do about it', after each short chapter.

In that sense, these are aimed more directly at practitioners than some of my longer form books, but there is a lot of cross over: there are a lot of big ideas in here, but I hope also a lot of things that you can action this afternoon!

These Guidebooks are not complete work, nor are they definitive 'answers'. But I hope they will inspire you to find your own answers: they will iterate over time, so do come back and check your version number to access the latest thinking.

Some of you may be familiar with my work already: I adhere to a methodology of #WorkingOutLoud, whereby all my work is shared openly, and as it takes shape. Where possible, I try to identify which bits of this work are stronger than others, and I share my mistakes and evolving understanding as well.

This work is grounded in my professional work through Sea Salt Learning: a global partner through change. Sea Salt Learning lets me engage in some of the key strategic challenges of our time, with some of the most incredible global Organisations. I am lucky to be immersed in a community of people who want to drive change. This holds my thinking, and work, to account, in a very direct way. It is to that community that I am directly responsible.

f you enjoy this work, please share it: I am always happy to engage in discussions with fellow Explorers of the Social Age.

- You can contact me on hello@seasaltlearning.com

- You can find out more about our work at Sea Salt Learning at www.SeaSaltLearning.com where we partner with Organisations through change, as well as finding details of the annual Certification programmes.

OVERVIEW

This short Guidebook is an exploration of *'Communities'*. It considers the key capabilities of the Social Leader as a Community Builder. It's about the communities that we build for Social Learning, that we engage with as Social Leaders, and that we will rely upon as we build our more Socially Dynamic Organisation.

It is intended to be both a space for thoughtful exploration, and a practical guide as to how you do it in practice. I've written it to help you to create the *'Conditions for Community'*: to support your work, whether it be to build new communities, to help existing ones grow and thrive, or to ensure that all of our communities are inclusive and interconnected. *'Interconnectivity'* is a core feature of the Socially Dynamic Organisation.

The context of this work is the Social Age: the evolved ecosystem in which we live (and the subject of another of these Guidebooks). Broadly speaking, the Social Age sees the rise of collectivism beyond traditional Organisational structures, facilitated by emergent and pervasive social collaborative technology, at radical scale, and existing outside the hierarchy of any formal organisational structure or rules. The communities that I describe here are not formal structures; they exist within the Social aspect of the Organisation.

Communities are our primary *'sense-making'* entities: we use them to discover new information, share knowledge, and figure out what on earth is happening in the noisy world around us. We are effective through our communities, and we are held in the arms of our communities.

This particular Guidebook draws upon a range of my writing on the blog, as well as two research projects, conducted through our Sea Salt Learning Research Hub: the first, *'The Landscape of Trust'*, is a global, ongoing, community-based research project that explores the nature of trust between individuals, within communities, and inside organisations. The second is a smaller scale research project, called *'Conditions for Community'*, conducted in conjunction with the NHS North West Leadership Academy.

THIS GUIDEBOOK IS STRUCTURED AS FOLLOWS:

1. *Foundations* of Community
2. *Barriers* to Community
3. What is *Community* for?
4. The ways that people *Connect*
5. *'Sense making'* in Communities
6. *Storytelling* in Communities
7. *Collaboration* in Communities
8. *Technology* in Communities
9. The *Timing* of Community

FOR EACH OF THESE AREAS:

- I provide a *high-level overview*
- I share *what the research shows us*, and provide my interpretation of these findings
- I've written guidance on *'what you can do about it'*
- I provide *links to additional resources*

It's valuable for us to shine a light into these spaces, to build an understanding of what are, at their core, complex social structures held together by a dynamic range of forces.

Specifically, *'Communities of Practice'* are central to our ability to be effective in the dynamic and adaptive knowledge environment of the Social Age.

If we can better understand the ways in which people connect, and engage, to learn, and support others in their learning, and how these social structures form, and are bonded, then we can better support this process.

'Support' is key; within the formal spaces of the organisation, we can *'own and control'* a given area, but as we venture deeper into *'social'* and emergent communities, we will see that much of the value comes from the semi-formal, socially moderated spaces. And to engage in these areas, we will need to nurture, recognise, respect, and support both individuals, and the value of the community itself. Indeed, we will have to work within the native rules of the system; it is not our place to impose rules upon it.

It's clear that learning communities are more than simply formal structures; they act at the intersection of knowledge and practice, and they move beyond simple transactional terms. Communities of Practice are about people.

For this reason, any guidance as to how we can better form, and utilise, Communities of Practice within an Organisational context, will inevitably need to move beyond simply looking at social collaborative technology, and formal, programmatic, approaches.

These learning communities are complex social systems, and to both understand them, and be effective within them, will require specific, socially moderated skills and behaviours. Capability that we can build for individual Social Leaders, and for Organisations themselves.

THE CONDITIONS FOR COMMUNITY

I sketched out 13 initial principles when I started trying to capture the conditions for community. These *'conditions'* form our foundations. It's not intended to be definitive, just part of a conversation about how *'community'* is more than simply *'technology'* or *'space'*. A brief overview would look like this:

- We need high SOCIAL CAPITAL: an ability to survive and thrive in social collaborative spaces. This is something that Social Leaders not only have themselves, but also that they develop in others. This should not be taken for granted, and encompasses much more than simply technical skills.

- There is value in having a DEMOCRATISED SPACE, which is space that is not owned purely by the organisation. In the Trust Research, we see that ownership of space significantly impacts engagement, so it's important to relinquish control if you want to earn the prize of engagement.

- We need clear RULES, ideally ones that are co-created, or at the very least, explicitly stated. Ambiguity leads to retrenched and safe behaviours, and not innovative or engaged ones.

- CONSEQUENCE is a powerful tool. I've been writing about 'the Sphere of Consequence' in 'Change' recently, and have come to realise that both the ownership of it, and its location, are important. When it comes to the triggering, format, permanence, and ownership, of consequence, clarity is key.

- We need strong SOCIAL LEADERSHIP in social communities. While at first this may seem obvious, the corollary is also true: we do not need an abundance of formal leadership. Leave formal power at the door.

- BROAD FAIRNESS is an organisation-wide need, but especially in communities: if the organisation has a culture that is not fair, then it cannot hear all the voices within the community that it needs to hear.

- We must have EQUAL OPPORTUNITY: opportunity to engage, to be heard, and to respond. This ties in with the ownership of stories. Communities are not broadcast spaces, they are co-creative ones.

- TRUST is central to coherent communities: focus on building strong, wide webs of social ties.

- A condition for the emergence of community is NEED, and not just need from the organisation, but need from individuals as well.

- Tied into the emergence of agility is the need for FLUIDITY OF ROLE: we cannot carry our formal role into a social space, and indeed, we see far greater fluidity of roles within these spaces anyway.

- While social communities may not need a PURPOSE per se, social communities within organisations probably should, even if the purpose of a Community of Practice is simply to support *'best practice'*, development, application, and reflection.

- We will find SHARED VALUES within our coherent communities, but we must first put in the effort: shared purpose can be imposed, but shared values must be found.

- Finally, SEGMENTED UTILITY: if we are all the same, our community will be weaker than if we have a broad and diverse range of skills, knowledge, and perspectives. The more segmented a community, but aligned through core, shared values, the stronger it will be.

I.
FOUNDATIONS
OF COMMUNITY

To consider *'Communities of Practice'* in the Social Age, we need to consider those that are formal, set up by the organisation, and those that are Social, emerging from within the broader community. We can therefore say that the foundations may be *'Formally'* or *'Socially'* moderated, with each type of community operating in different ways, serving different purposes, and operating within different power structures.

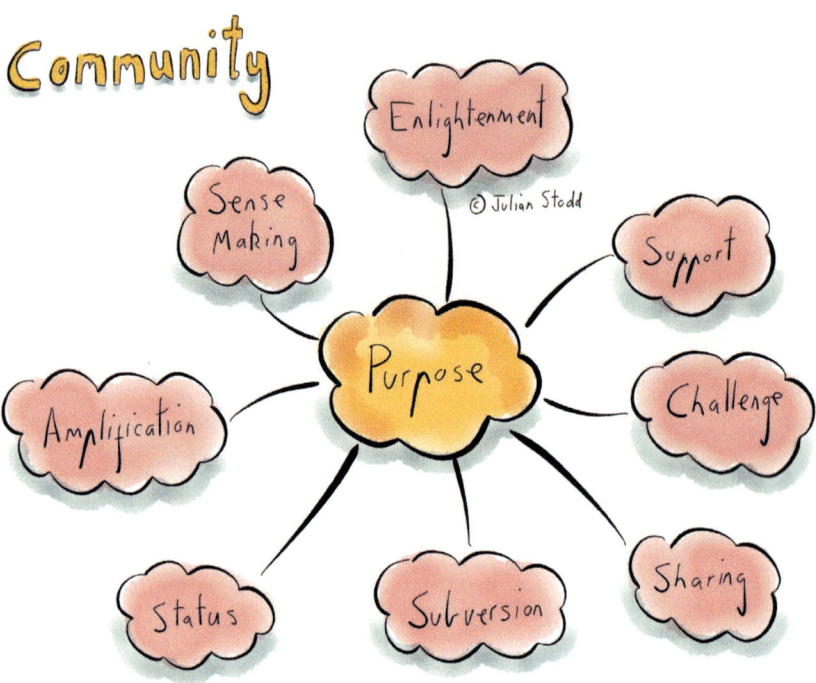

Communities serve many different purposes: some are *'sense-making'* entities, some offer *'support'*, some *'challenge'* their members, and others provide much needed *'subversion'* of established and dominant narratives, they exist to fracture the status quo. We belong to many different communities, some of which may hold conflicting views with each other.

Consider the foundations of community in terms of the environmental factors (such as the collaborative technology that they utilise, and the spaces that they inhabit), individual factors (such as individual Social Capital, levels of Social Leadership, and technological capability), and specific skills (such as storytelling, coaching, or community moderation).

One aspect to consider around the foundation of a given community is *'need'*: whether the community exists to serve a background need, or a specific project-based need, or something else entirely. This may relate to the life-cycle of the community: some communities are emergent, then disband rapidly, while others emerge and remain in perpetuity.

In my more recent work, I've started to consider a taxonomy of social structures, but I suspect that this work is just a diving off point for understanding this complex topic.

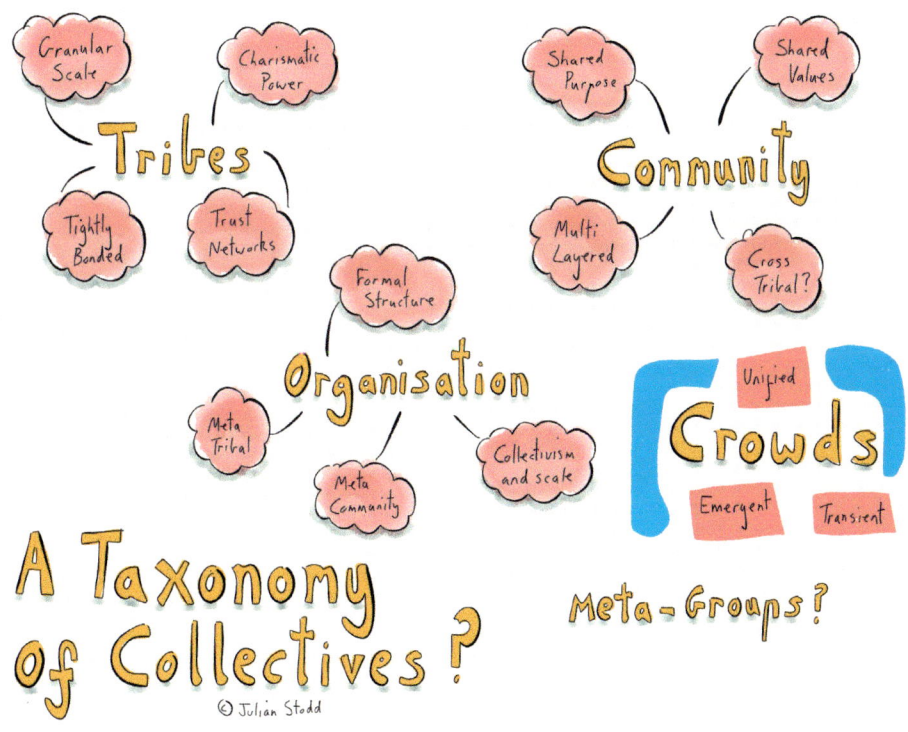

It looks at *'tribes'* as the strongest, *'trust-bonded'* social structure, and *'communities'* as meta-tribal structures, structures that draw upon one, or multiple, tribes. However, I suspect this is a vast oversimplification (as opposed to simply a useful abstraction). There are clearly different *'types'* of community, but equally the same group of people who form one *'community'* may manifest as an entirely different functional group, even simultaneously, within a different context.

So maybe, it's better to simply consider a functional taxonomy (e.g. group size and type of bonds) and a purposeful taxonomy (communities of challenge, support, subversion etc.). Or maybe I'm just overthinking it...

With regard to learning, individuals in Communities of Practice interact in different ways, and assume different roles as they do so. For many, their engagement is need-based, but it's clear that others derive significant tribal identity, and even self-actualisation, from their participation in their community.

WHAT DID THE RESEARCH SHOW?

- For nearly 63% of people, the Community of Practice that they most enjoyed participating in was informally created.

- For 54% of the population in the Landscape of Trust prototype study, the 'manifestation' of Trust, if the organisation trusted them, was 'Freedom'. Freedom to collectivise and explore.

- A Community was deemed to be more likely a loose association of volunteers (63.5%) than a formal structure.

- For 25% of respondents, there was no discernible leadership structure at all.

KEY THINGS TO REMEMBER:

- Some communities are 'formal', and many (most) are 'social'. You only own the formal ones.

- The motivation that people have to join a community may be diverse, and is not always clear, even to them. But whatever the motivation, 'membership' is a powerful force.

- We are effective 'within the arms of our community', but to be held in those arms is something that we earn, by investing in others, over time.

WHAT YOU CAN DO ABOUT THIS

Here are some things that you can do to give your Communities the best chance of success:

1. *Give people the means, permission, and support to create their own communities.*

2. *Worry less about what they may do wrong, and more about how you intend to listen to what they do right.*

3. *Consider potential points of tension, and try to proactively consider how you will handle dissent, avoiding imposing formal control upon the community at all costs.*

RESOURCES ON 'FOUNDATIONS'

The taxonomy of social structures:

https://julianstodd.wordpress.com/2017/11/03/tribes-communities-and-society-a-reflection-on-taxonomy/

A reflection on Social Leadership, looking at the importance of fairness, humility, and community:

https://julianstodd.wordpress.com/2018/02/12/social-leadership-fairness-humility-and-community/

An exploration of the role of ritual, and the cohesive forces of community:

https://julianstodd.wordpress.com/2017/09/05/rituals-artefacts-and-the-cohesive-forces-of-community/

Considering organisational resilience, and the links to community and power:

https://julianstodd.wordpress.com/2017/03/23/resilience-technology-community-and-power/

2.

BARRIERS TO COMMUNITY

Any particular community will have wide ranging barriers to entry, some of which are clear, and visible, and others of which are obscure, or deliberately hidden.

Formally moderated communities may have clear rules governing membership, as well as clear rules governing consequence and exclusion; by contrast, socially moderated communities rarely have such rules, and are instead governed by the community itself, established through social norms.

These *'normalised'* rules can uphold desirable traits, but may also reflect normalised bias and inequality. In the *'Landscape of Trust'* research, people described that 70% of the moderation of personal action was held in implicit rules, and only 30% in formal (written) ones. The ability to understand how these social rules (norms) are formed, and the impact of breaching them is a core part of being socially capable.

Normalisation is a mechanism by which aggregated social behaviours align, at scale, and can result in exclusion. There are a wide range of ways in which people can be excluded.

One of the most obvious mechanisms of exclusion is that people simply do not know that a specific community exists: they have a specific need, but no route into the community, or even knowledge of its existence.

Even if they do know that it exists, they may be excluded because they have no social connection into it, i.e. they cannot find the front door. Assuming it's even possible for them to get into the community, we have to remember that communities are social structures, and subject to the various biases and principles of exclusion that impact our wider society. So people may have the *'potential'* for access, but lack the *'permission'* to access.

People can be excluded because of age, gender, sexual preference, politics, technical ability, and a wide range of other sociological factors. They can also be excluded because their views do not align with those of the majority; even supposedly tolerant communities are typically tolerant only within certain limits. Indeed, all communities are exclusive once we move beyond their elastic limits.

In my wider writing, I have taken to using a bare bones definition of *'community'* as *'an entity of exclusion'*. By taking this rather more negative view, I am recognising that only some communities are held with shared values and shared purpose. Many exist almost entirely by excluding others.

WHAT DID THE RESEARCH SHOW?

- *Understanding the social zeitgeist of a community is particularly important for membership: 27% of people said that their ability to have a conversation in an online community depends on "how much I have 'gotten to know' those in the online community", which we could interpret to mean that you need to be accepted and included to engage.*

- *When it comes to the formal policy around engagement in online communities of practice, for 50% of respondents there was "no formal policy encouraging engagement".*

- *Only 15% of people said that they needed a "safe place to discuss challenges" to interact with their favourite community of practice, but of course that may be because they are already accepted and empowered.*

- *33% of respondents said that "a welcome from community participants" was what mattered most to them when joining a new community.*

- *43% of respondents strongly agreed with the statement "my work organisation welcomes difference" (in people, in ideas, in processes), but just over 28% either disagreed with this, or said it was "dependent" (on a contextualising factor).*

- *In our research for the NHS in Scotland, the cohort identified that the primary mechanism by which people were excluded from a community was 'lack of shared values and purpose'.*

All of these statistics present a pretty mixed picture; thus, we cannot assume that all communities are open to everyone.

For me, much of this impact lies in developing higher levels of Social Capital throughout the organisation by, for example, developing strong layers of Social Leadership, strong safeguards and support for Communities.

KEY THINGS TO REMEMBER:

- It's easy to consider communities in terms of consensus and unity, but remember that many are held together in opposition to something else.

- To be a member requires us to conform in specific ways: part of this conformity may lead to aggregated toxic behaviour.

- Communities are governed primarily by implicit, socially held, rules.

WHAT YOU CAN DO ABOUT THIS

Here are some things that you can do to remove barriers to a Community:

1. *Actively work out your rituals of engagement and departure: the role of ritual is something we understand well in our Social lives, and something we can mindfully develop in our workplaces.*

2. *Use storytelling activities (I share many examples of this on the blog, as well as a Social Leadership Certification in this) to drive that initial tribal engagement.*

3. *Actively monitor, and encourage groups to monitor, their makeup, and provide support around inclusion and diversity.*

RESOURCES FOR 'BARRIERS TO COMMUNITY'

An article explaining the *'sphere of consequence'*, one of the key moderators of individual engagement:

https://julianstodd.wordpress.com/2017/08/17/the-sphere-of-consequence/

Considering how culture fractures:

https://julianstodd.wordpress.com/2014/06/03/fractured-culture-exclusion/

And a piece on *'normalisation'*:

https://julianstodd.wordpress.com/2017/08/16/normalising-dolly/

Some early stage work that explores a model to understand the health of a community:

https://julianstodd.wordpress.com/2015/05/01/the-ceda-community-model-pt-2-engagement-permission-in-social-learning/

3.
WHAT IS COMMUNITY FOR?

What's a *'Community'* actually for? Does it have to have a purpose, or can it simply *'be'*? My own view is that communities are always bonded: either through shared purpose and intent, or in opposition to something else. Because they are, by definition, membership structures, something must differentiate *'membership'* from *'non-membership'*. Communities may emerge to service a particular need or have a particular conversation, or they may exist as a backbone to hold our *'connection'* safe, without any specific actionable purpose.

Within these varied communities, people carry out a wide range of conversations: sometimes through engagement with the whole community, but often within a subset of the community, partly determined by the technology with which they engage, and partly related to the sense of consequence, or exposure to risk, that they feel; the greater the sense of consequence, the more hidden the community is likely to be.

People in the research groups liked to talk about *'people'*. Indeed, the most popular keyword used when asking people about sense-making and pertinence was *'people'*, followed by *'community'*. They talked about *'online'* communities, *'faith'* communities, and *'cultural'* communities. They talked about *'young people'*, and 'inspiring people', as well as both *'leaders'* and *'peers'*. It is safe to say that a great deal of the conversation within a community is about the community, and that's probably to be expected.

Indeed, this constant dialogue about community is likely a self-reinforcing aspect of collective identity. Talking about our coherence may actually contribute to our coherence. We like to belong, and to reinforce that we belong, through words, rituals, costumes, and even artefacts like music. Nothing brings a group together like a shared anthem.

One important thing communities do is find their coherence, and they tend to do this in two key ways: firstly, they find a *consensus*, wherein people in the community come together and agree on something. Secondly, they unite in *dissent*, wherein people in the community come together in opposition to something else. In politics, we are currently seeing the widespread engagement of communities of dissent.

This represents a shift in my thinking: when I originally wrote the Social Leadership Handbook, I considered that *'shared purpose and values'* were the dominant force, but now I tend to consider that opposition and dissent may be more widespread.

The risks and benefits differ in both of these models of coherence: in terms of *'sense-making'*, Communities of Practice can be valuable to understand data and evolve professional practice by creating safe spaces to share and tell stories, and by being both empathic and supportive while we rehearse new behaviours and skills.

The risk comes through the monoculture makeup and nature of many communities, and hence forces of confirmation bias (whereby we hear voices that reinforce what we already believe to be true). Communities can end up holding a position of negative liberty: this is a position that serves the good of the community itself, and is misaligned with individual benefit. Therefore, if I join a community through an implicit social contract that it will also serve me, I may find myself caught in a Community that does not.

WHAT DID THE RESEARCH SHOW?

- Communities of Practice seem to stick 'on topic' pretty effectively: the majority of individuals who participated in the research identified as working primarily in 'healthcare', and the main concept they discussed was 'healthcare', followed by 'psychology', 'healthy', and 'community outreach'.

- The strongest utilised keywords were: 'words of improvement', 'community development', 'long-term impact', 'streamlining', 'training', and 'partnerships'.

- People were very clear about the specific benefits they received from the community interaction, which helps them understand the subject.

- They stated that 'knowledge' was the most important aspect, interestingly followed by 'hearing', which would seem to relate to the importance of communities as story-listening spaces.

- More widely, within my own global work on Social Leadership, we see that 'story listening' is often in the top three traits that people look for in their leaders.

- In an unpublished study, within a global tech company in 2017, over 5,000 participants identified 'Authentic Storytelling' as the number one thing they looked for in Social Leadership.

- Other important aspects of community interaction were: 'experience', 'understanding', 'challenge', and 'active listening'.

- These probably nicely reflect the 'sense-making' and 'developmental' aspects of community. Gaining access to other people's experiences and using the community to gain understanding can both help us achieve momentum.

- 'Challenge' is clearly important too, and active listening may relate nicely to what we saw elsewhere, which is that people want mentoring support to help them tell great stories.

- It's worth exploring the keywords that people used most often to describe the aspects of community interaction that help them understand the subject: 'people' and 'experiences'.

- Words around difference also occurred quite often: 'different perspectives' and 'a different point of view' indicate that people are actively looking for a range of opinions, at least in some cases.

KEY THINGS TO REMEMBER:

- *'Purpose' is important for action based communities, and it's not simply a function of formal ones.*

- *Communities may find coherence in their internal agreement, or they may find it in external dissent. Both are equally powerful (if you are interested in this, I have a series of articles on gang structures and violence that you may find interesting).*

- *Much of the conversation within a community may reinforce the social structure, and unique identity, of the community itself, but this is valuable, not just noise.*

WHAT YOU CAN DO ABOUT THIS

Here are some things that you can do to best support people in figuring out what their communities are for:

1. *Consider establishing a core set of formal communities, around specifi disciplines, but encourage the group to establish their conversational communities around the edges of these.*

2. *Be prepared to go where the conversation is, but only using your Socia Authority: don't wade in with formal power.*

3. *Carry out regular 'temperature checks' in your communities to capture the most popular topics that people are discussing; provide a narrative back into the community using the results.*

RESOURCES ON COMMUNITY

A reflection on communities that simply emerge:

https://julianstodd.wordpress.com/2016/06/30/emergent-community/

More early stage #WorkingOutLoud, considering aspects of moderation. Take this as part of an evolving body of work:

https://julianstodd.wordpress.com/2014/07/30/how-to-build-and-moderate-a-thriving-social-learning-community-part-1-forming/

Another early stage piece, considering the earliest days of a community:

https://julianstodd.wordpress.com/2015/06/24/social-learning-birth-of-a-community/

And see this work, which is a little more complex (as I evolve my own understanding), about gang structures. This work is really about power and consequence:

https://julianstodd.wordpress.com/2018/09/12/engaging-power-an-illustration-of-cohesion/

4.
WAYS THAT PEOPLE CONNECT

People exist within social systems. Inside these systems, we connect in a wide variety of ways, using a broad range of technologies. Sometimes, the context of the conversations dictates or defines the ways in which we connect; sometimes, our perception of consequence dictates the channel that we use. If we consider that the subject of our conversation is *'forbidden'*, then we are more likely to take the conversation to a safer space, perhaps using hidden technologies. Technologies that exist beyond the sight or control of the Organisation itself.

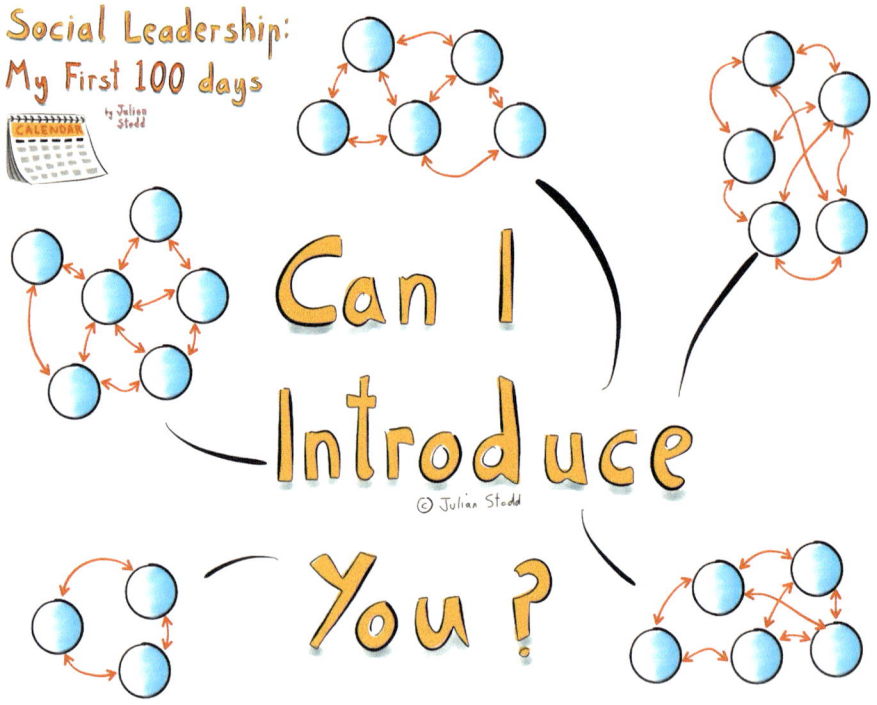

It's very clear that the conversations we have are far broader than any specific formal technology or formal space, and this clearly indicates the need for us to focus on the skills and capabilities of Social Leadership and community-based authority, even more so than formal leadership skills. To be effective, it is necessary for us to engage in multiple spaces, using different, contextual power.

When we look at the research results, there is a very clear emotional overtone to much of the language that people use when describing the communities to which they belong: people don't just express that they *'need'* to connect with others around a specific purpose, rather they use a range of other emotive language.

If you lack Social Capital, Technological Skills, or access to the technology itself, or if you lack explicit Permission or individual Impetus to connect, then you can be disenfranchised, and left out of the Community. Many of these things, like *'permission'* and *'technology'*, can be actively denied to us.

Even when we do have space and opportunity to connect, we may lack the Cultural Grammar to do so. Indeed, we may lack a full understanding of the rituals of engagement, the artefacts of power, or the shared social scripts that would enable us to join.

It's possible that there is a taxonomy of engagement as well, something along these lines:

- *Direct personal engagement, one-to-one*

- *Individual engagement, into an existing group*

- *Role-based engagement, to other roles*

- *Power-based engagement, into hierarchy*

- *Subversive engagement, outside the system*

- *Oppositional engagement, held against the system*

The ways in which we engage may relate closely to this taxonomy. Thus, how we engage in *'opposition'* likely differs from how we engage in *'consensus tribes'*.

I have found some aspects of this work particularly valuable: no matter how well connected we feel, it's worth remembering that most people overestimate how well connected and influential they are. We can always strive further to connect, not simply into communities with which we are comfortable and agree, but into communities of difference and dissent.

WHAT THE RESEARCH SHOWS

- 21% of people described being 'vouched in' to a community, as opposed to being able to access it through 'self-driven participation'.

- We know there are many different types of communities, and that not all are equally open. Indeed, some communities gain their internal coherence and value by being communities of status or communities defined by exclusion.

- The majority of people 'strongly agreed' that meeting face-to-face is important to building relationships; this is not atypical, but may simply represent that this is how we are used to doing things.

- While we can quantify that we forge online relationships differently from face-to-face ones, there may be nothing inherently 'bad' about forging relationships online. This is an area that I want to unpack further in future research.

- We could read this as a strong developmental need: how often is it practical to meet face-to-face and, possibly more importantly, if we just grow our communities through face-to-face interaction, are we building in greater bias and a stronger mono-culture?

- Whilst results have varied between different cohorts, people describe belonging to an average of 10-15 different communities.

KEY THINGS TO REMEMBER:

- *The ways that we connect are contextual: providing different context may, itself, provide new levels of connection.*

- *People describe that they are 'invited' into their most important communities, so we should consider the choreography of invitation.*

- *Communities are emotional spaces, not logical ones.*

WHAT YOU CAN DO ABOUT THIS

Here are some things that you can do to help people connect:

1. Consider regular sampling to see, for example, how many communities people are part of: if the results are broad, see if that correlates to demographics. Is part of your audience excluded?

2. Train specific capabilities around Social Leadership, the ability to understand how communities work, and how to join them.

3. Consider how you view Social Capital within the whole organisation; consider curating a conversation or a diagonal story across the organisation to explore how it currently sits.

RESOURCES RELATING TO 'CONNECTIVITY'

This piece considers how we create more trusted leadership:

https://julianstodd.wordpress.com/2017/12/07/leading-with-trust-a-development-pathway/

This key piece explores the notion of interconnectedness: how we link the different tribes:

https://julianstodd.wordpress.com/2017/11/23/not-one-but-many-the-interconnection-of-tribes/

This article explores the taxonomy of social collectivism:

https://julianstodd.wordpress.com/2017/11/03/tribes-communities-and-society-a-reflection-on-taxonomy/

This piece explores the scale of social systems:

https://julianstodd.wordpress.com/2017/10/18/the-scale-of-social-systems-tribes-and-tribes-of-tribes/

Finally, this piece looks at a culture of sharing as one component of Social Leadership:

https://julianstodd.wordpress.com/2014/10/17/building-a-culture-of-sharing/

5.

SENSE MAKING
COMMUNITIES

Our ability to make sense of things, to filter out the signal from the noise, is vital for Social Leaders, who operate in dynamic and cluttered environments. In the Social Age, knowledge itself is no longer enough: it's our ability to do something with it that counts, and that ability is often enhanced by the community that surrounds us.

It's not just the context of knowledge that has changed, it's the nature of knowledge itself: while we still rely on certain fixed types of knowledge, in our everyday lives much of the knowledge that we engage with is substantially co-created, dynamic, adaptive, and evolutionary.

To be effective, we must utilise both types of knowledge: the fixed knowledge that we learn through formal programmes, and the co-created knowledge that we access through our communities.

Communities do not simply facilitate the transmission of fixed knowledge, they can act as active *'sense-making'* entities, through mechanisms of social filtering, contextualising, and amplification.

Social filtering is a type of aggregated understanding, whereby individuals each provide context on a specific subject and collectively create a narrative around it.

There is a great deal of noise about *'fakery and bias'* right now, and while these are legitimate concerns, it is a mistake to imagine that these are new problems that we have accidentally created; we haven't. We have merely shined a light on the long-term bias within the system. Both competence in gauging validity and fact-checking form core skills for communities to deploy. The *'echo chamber'* is not a piece of technology; rather, it's a human habit that is demonstrated through technology. To fix it, fix the behaviour (imagining it needs to be *'fixed'*; more likely, we just need more meaningful conversations about provenance, bias, and *'fact'*).

The contextualisation of knowledge is about the community of practitioners that surround us, with a shared understanding of the context of our everyday work, and the ability to contextualise new knowledge within it.

Social Amplification is the mechanism whereby important knowledge, and highly authentic stories, can be amplified through community. Thus, amplification is a function of the strength of connection, but also, crucially, the diversity of our connections.

Monoculture communities will be less effective at amplification than diversified and highly interconnected ones.

WHAT DID THE RESEARCH SHOW?

- *People described the way in which the community gave them access to 'knowledge', but importantly also 'experience', 'understanding', 'challenge', and that the community 'actively listened'.*

- *When asked about the need to learn something new related to work, 44% of people claimed that they would ask their community of practice, which is, incidentally, exactly twice as many who said they would "look for it on Google".*

- *Respondents talked about how the community gave them 'different perspectives': for 33% of people, the fact that a community of practice 'crosses between areas of practice' is specifically important.*

- *They described a 'safe non-judgemental space' and the experience of 'cross sector people', which ties into the importance of diversification of community and the ability to hear a wide range of voices.*

- *That community spaces are non-judgemental is extremely important: in the Landscape of Trust work, and research into Co-Created change, I have found that consequence is a dominant force that can silence curiosity.*

- *People 'strongly agreed' that 'space' and 'time' are important for reflection, which is probably a policy and mindset issue that may need to be addressed. As we move towards more social models of learning and performance, we may have to address scheduling and allocation, or even ownership, of our time.*

KEY THINGS TO REMEMBER:

- *The nature of knowledge has changed: work hard to understand how 'validation' has shifted, and the impact of this for Organisational learning.*

- *Communities act as social filters: so diversify your communities. With only one filter, you can only remove one bias.*

- *The formal knowledge that Organisations impart may be viewed as half of what we need.*

WHAT YOU CAN DO ABOUT THIS

Here are some things that you can do to support Community *'sense-making'*:

1. *Consider using a social currency to recognise expertise.*

2. *Consider establishing an alumni network.*

3. *Consider using crowd-sourcing for problem-solving; tap into the 'sense-making' community, but be sure to offer a socially moderated reward!*

RESOURCES ON 'SENSE-MAKING'

A reflection on tacit and tribal knowledge:

https://julianstodd.wordpress.com/2015/09/21/tacit-and-tribal-knowledge-socially-moderated-sense-making/

A piece exploring how social systems are not simply complex: they are radically complex, especially as they scale:

https://julianstodd.wordpress.com/2017/07/05/a-state-of-radical-complexity/

One of a range of pieces exploring *'currency'*. This is one of the areas I'm focussing on right now in my practice: recognising, and building out, multiple currencies of recognition and reward:

https://julianstodd.wordpress.com/2018/02/14/the-currency-of-social-engagement-moderation-and-validation-of-reward/

6.
STORYTELLING IN COMMUNITIES

Within our communities, we share stories: stories of unity, stories of dissent, stories of pride and of belief. Stories form the basic mechanism for the transmission of cultural information and knowledge. In the Social Age, stories are more important than ever.

Within an organisation, stories battle it out for supremacy; strive to gain the upper hand, are sometimes shared widely, and sometimes appropriated and reshaped by the recipient. Stories are fluid, adaptive, and way beyond our ability to control.

In my own work, I have identified three layers of storytelling that are relevant to social sense-making communities: the *'Individual Stories'* that are formed and shared by each participant, the *'Co-Created Stories'* that are written by the community itself with the input of many, and the *'Organisational Stories'* that form a formal narrative and are owned and controlled by the organisation itself.

There is a natural tension between these three types of stories: personal narratives are typically deemed to be highly authentic, and authenticity is typically the number one thing that people look for in stories. Therefore, by default, we greatly value individual stories. Co-Created narratives typically do not share a story of consensus: it is rare, and not necessarily valuable, for a community to have a unified opinion about something. Instead, Co-Created narratives are often stories of difference. Indeed, learning to shape and share these *'stories of difference'* can be a specific skill that should be developed within communities.

Organisational stories are typically highly formal: they will often have high production value, and are both owned and controlled by the organisation itself. They may tolerate limited dissent from the established narrative.

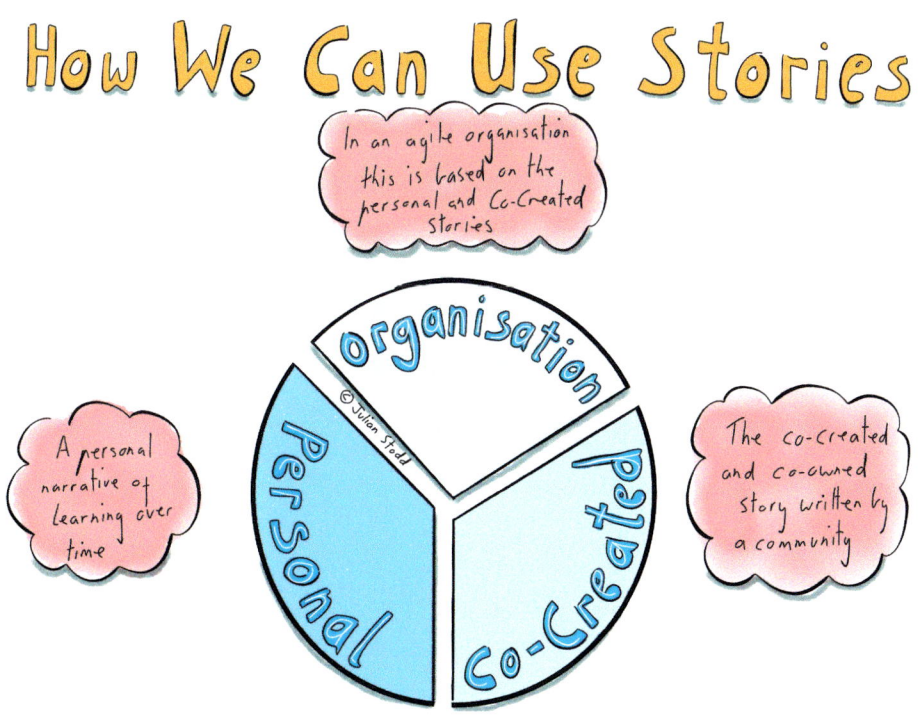

How We Can Use Stories

In an agile organisation this is based on the personal and Co-Created stories

A personal narrative of learning over time

The co-created and co-owned story written by a community

Organisation
Personal
Co-Created

© Julian Stodd

As we explore online and emergent Learning Communities, we would expect to see a greater emphasis on both *'Individual'* and *'Co-Created'* storytelling, with formal *'Organisational'* narratives being somewhat less relevant, because Organisational narratives tend to be broadcast, while community spaces tend to be collaborative and co-creative.

It's hard to look at stories without considering the underlying type of power behind them: organisational stories carry the weight of the organisation, while individual narratives carry the authenticity of the individual.

Co-Created narratives, by contrast, carry the power of reputation and consensus, which is why they can take longer to form. However, when they do form, they can carry great persistence.

'Storytelling' is what we do, at scale, within communities. Thus, it is worthwhile to invest in understanding how stories work, how they are owned, and how they are controlled.

THE NEW YORK DERELICTION WALK

AN EXPLORATION OF DERELICTION, FAILURE, INNOVATION, AND SOCIALLY CO-CREATED CHANGE.

AN EXPERIMENTAL PROJECT BY JULIAN STODD

CONTACT HELLO@SEASALTLEARNING.COM
FOR MORE INFORMATION, AND A COPY OF THE ROUTE MAP.

Recently I have been using language around *'Dominant Narratives'*, which is a term that came out of the *'New York Dereliction Walk'* that I ran last year: it's a term to describe *'how things are'*. The established, and commonly held, sense of normal. For example, our current view of same sex marriage is a *'dominant narrative'* that has recently evolved.

Understanding how dominant narratives are held, and how they evolve, seems to be essential to understand change. Storytelling is part of this, and hence the communities in which it happens are important. If you are particularly interested in this, I've shared the full text of the Dereliction Walk over on the blog.

One more thing to consider: last year I wrote a piece on the *'violence'* of stories: remember that every story, no matter how gently we tell it, carries a certain violence within it. Our stories of well-intentioned action may nonetheless exclude others, especially if we lack the space to listen.

WHAT DID THE RESEARCH SHOW?

- *When asked, 'what would help you to tell a story', 19% of people answered 'mentoring to boost confidence in how to do it'.*

- *Only one person wanted to see an example of a good story.*

- *21% of people wanted to set time aside to tell stories.*

- *16% of people said that 'tools' would help them tell a story (another area that will be interesting to unpack further). Is this specifically about technologies for storytelling or access to resources, or something deeper even, where 'tools' are used as a proxy for 'permission'?*

- *Approximately 15% of people stated that their favourite community of practice encourages 'sharing stories of success'.*

EY THINGS TO REMEMBER:

- *'Dominant Narratives' are the commonly held delusions by which we understand the world. To understand this is to understand change.*

- *I describe three levels of narrative: Individual, Co-Created, and Organisational. The trick is to understand how each influences the other.*

- *Remember that storytelling 'in' a community is very different from storytelling 'between' communities.*

WHAT YOU CAN DO ABOUT STORYTELLING

Here are some things that you can do around 'Storytelling' in communities:

1. *Create a layer of Social Storytellers and offer them even more opportunity to develop their skills.*

2. *Build the capability to tell 'stories of difference', and look at the underlying need for foundations of respect.*

3. *Consider building the Story Listening skills of your leaders.*

RESOURCES FOR STORYTELLING

For better or worse, some ideas I've shared on storytelling!

https://julianstodd.wordpress.com/2018/02/13/storytelling-session-ideas-workingoutloud/

'Cultural Graffiti' is something I've found to be one of my most useful new ideas: it's a way of exploring unheard wisdom, hidden voices. This is the first time I've put the work on *'graffiti'* into practice:

https://julianstodd.wordpress.com/2018/03/05/cultural-graffiti/

Another emergent piece here: I think that the skills of Story Listening are vital to develop, especially in more senior leadership. This is a key evolution of my own work in the last two years:

https://julianstodd.wordpress.com/2017/09/18/story-listening/

A piece about the evolution of dominant narratives:

https://julianstodd.wordpress.com/2017/08/18/nationhood-statues-salutes-and-narratives-of-power/

'Stories of Difference' is a specific technique I use to explore difference within intact groups. You can read about it here:

https://julianstodd.wordpress.com/2018/12/11/stories-of-dissent/

A reflection on gun control, which is a case study for understanding *'Dominant Narratives'*:

https://julianstodd.wordpress.com/2018/02/22/gun-control-a-case-study-in-authenticity/

7.

COLLABORATION IN COMMUNITIES

It's easy to collaborate with those people with whom you agree, to tackle known challenges, within a known context. But we may need to collaborate in complex contexts, across our differences, and face unknown challenges, in unknown spaces. Complex collaboration may well be a differentiating skill for Social Leaders.

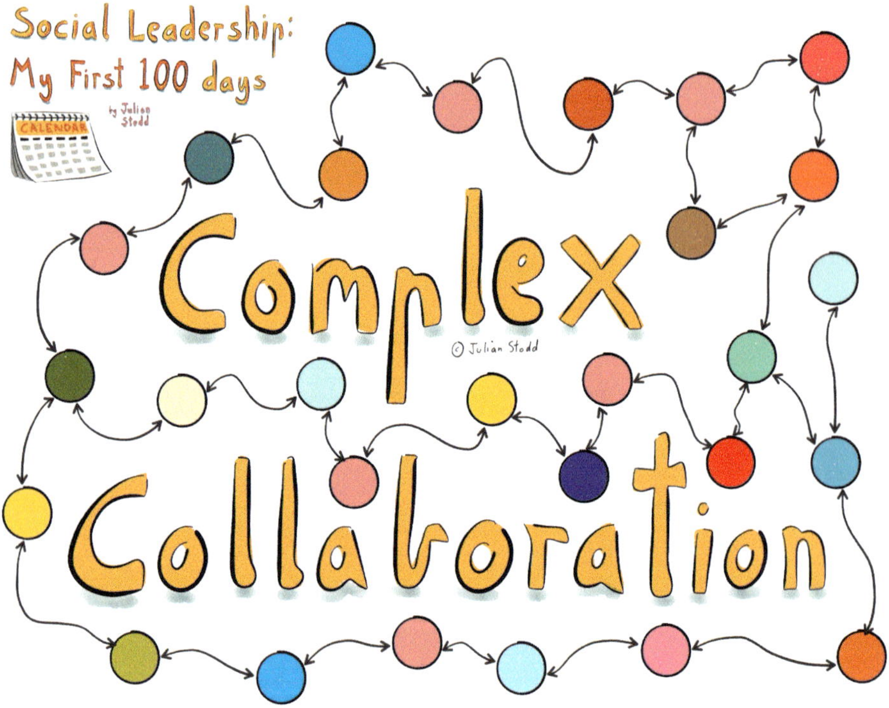

Collaboration is hard; a group of people thrust together does not entail collaboration, nor is collaboration simply a matter of giving people collaborative technology and beautifully decorated spaces. Indeed, we often see that collaboration occurs in opposition to established systems, outside formal technologies, and in extremely trying conditions.

Collaborating with known people, to achieve known ends, is not difficult. But to face the types of challenges we face today, against the backdrop of the Social Age, in a time of constant change, often within deeply fragmented and fractured cultures, we need to engage across our differences, and with a strong foundation of respect, to achieve complex collaboration.

There is an intersection between collaboration and bias: forces of confirmation bias and unconscious bias can contribute towards us building communities of similarity, and ones that are not just similar in makeup, but in thought itself. We build groups that look like us and think like us to reinforce what we already know to be *'true'*.

Thus, the skills that we need to foster, to forge more complex collaboration by building more diversified and interconnected communities, may well be the same skills we need to drive towards greater inclusion and lower bias.

If we wish to create collaborative communities, we need to invest in them: not money, but energy, permission, and freedom—the forces that are valued by the community itself.

WHAT THE RESEARCH SHOWS

- When we asked people about community interaction, 'good ground rules' was one of the strong phrases mentioned.

- While people wanted 'a different point of view' and 'different perspectives', they also wanted collaboration to happen in 'safe non-judgemental spaces' with 'good community support'.

- In the CEDA Survey, we explicitly looked at 'debate', which is part of both sense-making and collaboration.

- One interesting result related to whether people identified as 'gregarious' or 'reserved': 60% of respondents said that they were 'a mix of both gregarious and reserved', while 40% identified themselves solely as 'gregarious', and none identified themselves as reserved.

- This relates to a wider debate about whether communities, especially online Communities of Practice, are the domain predominantly of extroverts.

- Within Social Leadership work, it seems clear that people take a broad range of roles within their social communities, some of which are more traditionally extrovert, while some are more empathic, nurturing, and developmental.

- Still, this is almost certainly an area to benefit from deeper research: if we are simply enabling and empowering extroverts, then we are unintentionally disenfranchising and disempowering those whose voices are quieter.

- Feedback can be important; one question that explored this in detail raises some specific challenges: we asked people, 'if someone gives me negative feedback on a task, project, or idea I have, I am more likely to respond positively to that feedback if…', and 60% of people answered 'provided by a friend, face-to-face', while only 20% responded to feedback 'from a boss, face-to-face', and 20% said 'provided by a group I solicited for feedback, face-to-face'.

- Trust is an important aspect of our willingness to accept feedback, although this idea of only soliciting feedback from friends leaves us at risk of confirmation bias.

KEY THINGS TO REMEMBER:

- *Simple collaboration may not be enough. But complex collaboration is... complicated.*

- *The safety of the space that we disagree in is deemed important.*

- *There is a specific capability to collaborate, but it's more nuanced than simply being gregarious or confident. Seek to understand this, and put it (Social Capital) at the heart of your leadership development approach.*

WHAT YOU CAN DO ABOUT COLLABORATION

Here are some things that you can do to give your communities the best chance of collaborating at scale:

1. *Set strong ground rules, or, even better, co-create the ground rules for full shared ownership with the community.*

2. *Address 'how to give feedback'; consider a development track around this. Also, 'how to take feedback', and sit in discomfort.*

3. *Trust is key: look at strategies for building Trusted Leaders.*

RESOURCES ON COLLABORATION

Forgive me shamelessly sharing a development path for *'Leading with Trust'*. However you do it, a structured developmental approach is likely to be valuable:

https://julianstodd.wordpress.com/2017/12/07/leading-with-trust-a-development-pathway/

A foundational premise: that we must collaborate in complex ways. Note that this work built out of my exploration of *'Innovation'* in 2017, and continues to evolve:

https://julianstodd.wordpress.com/2017/03/29/complex-collaboration/

Foundation piece on why we need trust in Organisations:

https://julianstodd.wordpress.com/2017/11/10/the-need-for-trust/

8.
TECHNOLOGY
& COMMUNITY

The relationship between *'technology'* and *'community'* is a rather complex one; it can be easiest to consider in terms of *'conversations'* and *'spaces'*. Conversations take place within certain spaces, but we must not mistake the space for the conversation: conversations are fluid, and therefore able to move around, and even between, spaces.

You want *'conversation'* as this is part of sense making, but Organisations often focus on the place where the conversation takes place. And when they measure, they often do so within simply one space, whilst conversations flow between many: this is a core weakness in social network analysis tools. They measure the visible space, but this is only a subset of the total space.

Within the context of *'communities'*, we can consider technology to be the buildings that make up a village; however, the conversations are what make it a community. You can build as many houses and shops as you like, but until people stand outside the bakery and have a conversation about you, it's simply architecture.

Even within this context, we can differentiate between different types of technology: by considering the formality of the technology, the ownership of it, and the permanence of the stories told within it.

The *'formality'* of technology is like a totem; it is a code for *'ownership and control'*. If you, as the Organisation, provide the technology, then inherently you *'own'* it, and inherently I will behave in specific ways within it (much as we see people behave differently in office spaces and social spaces. Except maybe at Christmas Parties...).

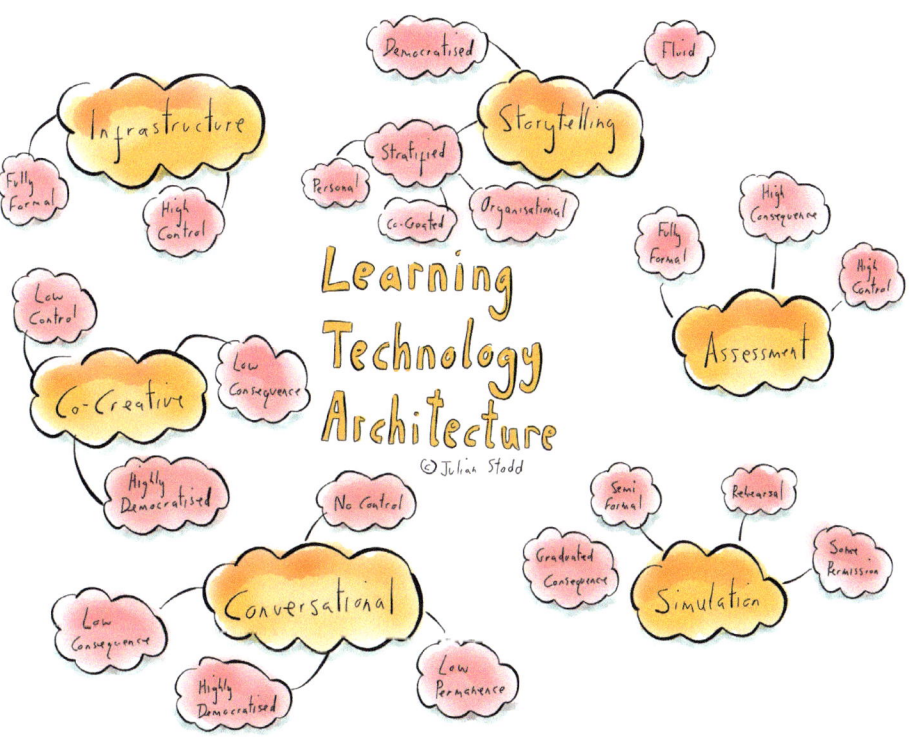

Normally I would recommend adopting a broad and diverse ecosystem of technology. In my Learning Technology architecture work, I discuss segregating spaces, and considering the formality, permanence, and democratisation, of each.

For example, *'Conversational'* spaces should be synchronous, disposable, and highly democratised, whilst *'Assessment'* spaces should carry high consequence, and are fully owned. This map just represents my own understanding: you don't need to use this one, but I would recommend that you segregate and differentiate the space, and don't try to own it all.

WHAT DID THE RESEARCH SHOW?

Note that the group surveyed here were from a single large Organisation, so specific technologies they mention may be less important, but I felt it was valuable to include it for the overarching points that it makes. And you could repeat the research in your own Organisation to measure against this baseline.

- *We were able to see clearly differentiated usage of technology between 'formal' and 'social' spaces.*

- *People used call conferencing more than four times as often at work than at home.*

- *Email was used similarly at home and at work.*

- *The democratisation of infrastructure technology makes it unsurprising that video conferencing was used widely in both 'formal' and 'social' contexts (25% higher in formal contexts), although still notably low overall, just 12% of the total.*

- *Instant messaging was used by almost twice as many people at home than at work, despite many organisations investing in social collaborative technologies.*

- *Within this healthcare-focused population, email still seems the dominant technology; synchronous and semi-permanent.*

- *When more broadly examining the online spaces that people used, Twitter, Facebook, LinkedIn, and YouTube are the top four spaces.*

- *WhatsApp rated very low (under 1% socially), with just over 2% in formal collaboration. I suspect that this will correlate to a wider difference in the age-related uptake of specific technologies, or perhap predictable patterns of innovation and adoption.*

- *When we asked the follow-up question regarding whether individuals had used these channels for online collaboration, the results were broadly 50% or less for all channels, with only one exception.*

- *SharePoint was the only technology identified that is used more widely as a 'formal' collaborative tool, as opposed to an online 'social' collaboration space.*

- *This result should be unsurprising, because SharePoint is offered in the market as an organisational collaboration tool, not a social collaboration tool in a democratised sense. It also requires significant configuration, cost, and back-end support, in contrast to most typical collaboration tools (e.g. Google Docs).*

- *The level of collaboration may indicate positive uptake, or it may indicate that a great deal of collaboration is carried out illicitly elsewhere, and may not show up in the data.*

- *Or, indeed, may represent a vast potential for collaboration that is simply not happening at all!*

KEY THINGS TO REMEMBER

- *Community may provide the 'space', but it does not make it a 'place'.*

- *Ownership of the space is a dominant influence on behaviour within it.*

- *Social technologies are viewed as semi disposable, and a diverse ecosystem is the strongest approach.*

WHAT YOU CAN DO ABOUT TECHNOLOGY

Here are some things that you can consider about technology:

1. *Evolve nuanced approaches to ownership and control: have rules that fit behaviours unless there is a clear and transparent reason to try to shift behaviours (e.g. 'control' is not enough, nor is blind conversation about 'risk').*

2. *Consider democratising aspects of your technology investment.*

3. *Build capability within your tech team, and wider organisation, to crowd-source potential new technology; move beyond 'not invented here'.*

RESOURCES ON TECHNOLOGY

occasionally redraw this map to represent the domains of Learning Technology see as most active:

https://julianstodd.wordpress.com/2017/02/02/learning-technology-map-2017/

---

gain, a reflection on social structures, and how they are impacted by echnology:

https://julianstodd.wordpress.com/2018/01/09/modes-of-social-organisation-by-he-people-for-the-people/

---

pecifically considering technology as a mechanism of control:

https://julianstodd.wordpress.com/2016/07/27/technology-as-control-vorkingoutloud/

9.
THE TIMING OF COMMUNITY

Typically, we see that both the formation of, and engagement within, communities correlates closely with both the tempo of activity and the synchronicity of participant engagement.

Communities that have some kind of imposed tempo will do quite well: specific topics that are being discussed weekly, a pattern of online and off-line activities, celebration of specific acts of graduation or achievement, etc.

You can achieve engagement by creating this tempo, and even by time limiting access to certain resources: scarcity seems to count!

Similarly, communities may have an internal tempo—one that is predominantly driven by active discussion around hot topics. However, whether the tempo is internal or external, synchronicity is important.

If people come across a conversation that has lain inactive for a long period of time, the information may be outdated. If people are within a conversation where others are slow to respond, they may lose interest. This probably relates to the underlying neurology of engagement, where every response makes us feel good in a timely manner, and not simply because people agree with us, but often because it enables us to re-enter the fray!

It shouldn't be surprising then, that a feature of interpersonal, face-to-face conversations is synchronicity, and this is equally true in online spaces.

WHAT DID THE RESEARCH SHOW?

- 57% of people said that the last time 'the last time I participated in a favourite community of practice' was "today".

- Moreover, 14% of people responded that it was "yesterday".

- The fact that nearly 29% of people said that the last time they had participated was a month ago may indicate one of two things: it may be that people are generally very engaged in their communities, although equally it may reflect that people who are very engaged in their communities are more likely to participate in communities of practice research!

- An alternative view is that this high engagement correlates to the fact that 62% of people most enjoyed participating in communities that were informally created.

- In other words, informally created communities may generally exhibit high levels of synchronous, or near synchronous, engagement.

- Another interesting feature is that over 70% of participants identified as being self-driven in their participation, and that motivation may also mean that they will be less happy if there is no response.

KEY THINGS TO REMEMBER:

- *Tempo is important, and may be internally generated, or externally imposed.*

- *Scarcity may act as a driver of engagement: time limit some access.*

- *People report that they are very engaged: if your own community is not highly engaged, ask people where they are going instead!*

WHAT YOU CAN DO ABOUT TIMING

Here are some things that you can do to help your communities with time:

1. *As uptake seems widespread, focus efforts to identify those who are left behind.*

2. *Consider socially moderated and validated badges of engagement.*

3. *Review all of your formal spaces, with the aim of understanding whether moderation and response are synchronous enough: if not, fix it or lose the space.*

RESOURCES ON MOMENTUM AND AMPLIFICATION

The details of this piece may not be perfect, but I think the approach is simple and significant: consider how you form, guide, and narrate your community:

https://julianstodd.wordpress.com/2013/02/28/the-lifecycle-of-a-social-learning-community-and-the-shape-of-moderation/

A broader piece about the Social Age, and the importance of community:

https://julianstodd.wordpress.com/2017/09/22/10-truths-at-the-start-of-the-social-age/

I share this one again, as it relates to synchronicity of response: these social movements happen because they have a tempo:

https://julianstodd.wordpress.com/2018/02/22/gun-control-a-case-study-in-authenticity/

SUMMARY

We live in the Social Age; our ability to lead, learn, and be effective, is largely rooted in our ability to engage with many and varied communities. However, since communities are complex social structures, our views towards them should be nuanced, and move beyond simple control.

The Communities research highlights a sophisticated set of behaviours and competencies that lead to the *'high-functioning'* nature and social value of these types of communities. These are factors that we cannot take for granted.

The behaviours exhibited, the ways that people engage, their approach to consequence, the impacts of technology etc, are learned over time, often through mistakes, and are not equally held. Some people are more successful at finding and accessing communities, partly through intrinsic nature, and partly because they fit the dominant, normalised model. Hence, the corollary is true: some people are disenfranchised and discriminated against in this new world because they lack the capability, or permission, to engage.

Any approach we take towards establishing and supporting Learning Communities within an organisation must be comprehensive, but must also recognise the inherent differences between the following four concepts:

1. *Formal is a term that defines formally established and owned communities, with formal edges, and formal power structures: we can do what we like with these.*

2. *Social is a term that defines socially established communities, with distributed ownership (and power) structures, to whatever extent they exist.*

3. *Spaces are the places where conversations take place. Very few conversations are available only in one space: As a rule, conversations move across multiple spaces, and are outside our direct control.*

4. *Permission may be granted, or claimed, which is why rule-based approaches to community, even in formal spaces, will have a limited effect.*

For every piece of energy, every conversation, that you can see, you will not be able to see the majority of energy. Don't mistake visibility for activity, or visibility for ability to control.

We have explored a range of aspects of Communities, specifically Communities of Practice, and considered aspects of their complexity, functioning, and development. As communities are inherently about people, focus your investment in people.

The research I've shared here is from a variety of sources: the global *'Landscape of Trust'* research, and several iterations of the *'Communities of Practice'* work. But there is no substitute for engaging with your own population, and generating your own baseline.

Complex social systems are radically complex systems that will always flow through our fingers. They fundamentally differ from the formal structures of teams and domains with which we are more familiar.

Our best bet is to learn how communities work in our own organisations, and to focus our efforts on diagnostics, temperature checks, and sampling approaches that allow us to visualise and learn what is really happening, as opposed to blindly seeking to replicate outdated models of formal power and control.

THE GUIDEBOOK SERIES

I've written a series of *'Guidebooks'* for the Social Age: these cover aspects of my work that are still rapidly evolving, or which I have not made time to write a full book about yet. They are typically under 10k words, and are intended to provide an overview of the landscape. I try to keep them practical, with a key highlight on *'what you need to know'*, and *'what you can do about it'*.

'The Social Learning Guidebook' provides a practical overview for the principles and design techniques of Social Learning in a modern organisation.

'The Learning Science Guidebook' is a practical, pragmatic, exploration of learning science, and helps you to curate your own discipline as a Learning Scientist. It looks at how learning can be evidence based, research led, and truly effective.

'The Trust Guidebook' explores our extensive research into the Landscape of Trust, and asks 72 questions that leaders can use with their teams.

'The Community Builder Guidebook' brings you practical ideas to create engaged and dynamic Social Learning Communities and Communities of Practice.

'The Social Age Guidebook' provides a comprehensive exploration of our new environment of work, and highlights key areas where Organisations need to adapt.

'The Storytelling Guidebook' provides an overview of how stories work and how Social Leaders become Authentic Storytellers.

'The New York Dereliction Walk' is more experimental work, exploring how Organisations and ideas fall derelict and fail, but can be reborn through social movements. It was my favourite writing from 2018.

'To the Moon and Back: Leadership Reflections from Apollo' shares eight key stories about the Apollo programme, alongside my personal reflection on what this means for Leadership in the Social Age.'

THE HANDBOOK SERIES

'*Handbooks*' are intended to capture a full snapshot of my evolving body of work on a particular subject. '*The Social Leadership Handbook*', now in it's second edition, explores the intersection of Formal and Social authority, and considers the importance of this in the context of the Social Age.

I'm currently finishing writing '*The Change Handbook*', to be published in 2019, which is an exploration of how Organisations change, and the forces that hold them constrained. It considers how we build more Socially Dynamic Organisations.

THE '100 DAY', AND 'SKETCHBOOK', SERIES

Whilst *'Handbooks'* and *'Guidebooks'* are about ideas and strategy, the *'100 Day'* books tackle how we do these things at scale. They do so by providing a scaffolded space, which you can explore, document, and graffiti, as you go.

'Social Leadership: My First 100 Days' is a practical, guided, reflective journey. It follows 100 days of activity, with each day including provocations, questions, and actions. You fill in the book as you go. It's accompanied by a full set of 100 podcasts.

'The Trust Sketchbook' is another guided, reflective journey, a walk through the Landscape of Trust, but in this case you graffiti and adapt the book, to capture your own landscape.

OTHER BOOKS

I have written a series of other books, covering aspects of learning, culture, technology, and knowledge, which you can find details of on the blog.

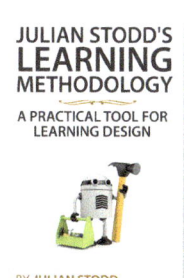

CERTIFICATIONS

In 2018 I launched the first Certification programme on *'Storytelling in Social Leadership'*. It's based upon *'Foundations'* and *'Techniques'*, which are practical and applied, and *'Experiments'*, which you learn to run in your own Organisation.

Throughout 2019 and 2020, the Certification offering is growing rapidly to include:

'Storytelling in Social Leadership'   *'Modern Learning Capabilities'*

'Leading with Trust'   *'Leading Through Change'*

'Community Building'   *'Social Age Navigation'*

'Foundations of Social Leadership'   Get in touch to find out more.

MOOCS AND PODCASTS

I run two MOOCs, one on *'Foundations of the Social Age'*, and one to accompany *'Social Leadership: My First 100 Days'*. You can find details at www.seasaltlearning.com, or drop me a line.

I publish occasional podcasts, on all aspects of my work. You can find me through your usual podcast player.

THE BLOG AND THE CAPTAIN'S LOG

I write the blog every day, sharing my current thinking and illustrations. You can find it at www.julianstodd.wordpress.com

I write a weekly newsletter for Social Age Explorers: it comments on news items, from the perspective of the Social Age, as well as providing expanded commentary around my own writing and thinking. Visit www.bit.ly/TheCaptainsLog to sign up.

SEA SALT LEARNING ⚓

In a more formal space, I founded Sea Salt Learning in 2014, acting as a global partner for change. We help some of the biggest and most interesting Organisations in the world get fit for the Social Age, through strategic consulting, building capability in teams, and building programmes to reach out at scale.

ABOUT SEA SALT LEARNING

We are a dynamic *Social Age startup:* five years old, living the values we speak. We are virtualised, global, inclusive, and agile. We are a core team of around twenty Crew Mates.

We are surrounded by a much larger layer of Social Age *'Explorers'*, people who are heavily involved in *'sense making'* around our core topics of Social Learning, Social Leadership, Change, Culture, and the Socially Dynamic Organisation.

Sea Salt Learning builds upon the work by Julian Stodd, author and explorer of the Social Age, recognised for his pioneering work in helping organisations to adapt to the new reality of the Social Age.

The *Sea Salt Research Hub* carries out original, creative, and large scale research, providing an evidence base for our work.

Sea Salt Publishing provides a curated body of books and online publications, exploring all aspects of the Social Age.

Sea Salt Digital provides our technical capability and build capacity for eLearning, mobile, video, and other forms of online learning.

THE EXPLORER COMMUNITY

All alumni of Sea Salt Learning programmes join our global community of Explorers. This gives access to all of our Open Sessions, as well as dedicated Explorer events, webinars, and networking.

It's an open community, dedicated to exploring all aspects of the Social Age: membership is free, based on foundations of respect and sharing, celebrating diversified views.